Hold Tight to your Faith

Nikki M. Crutchfield

Words N Wisdom Publishing
Beltsville, MD

Nikki Crutchfield/Words N Wisdom Publishing
www.wordsnwisdom.com
words_n_wisdom@yahoo.com
All biblical references are from the Holy Bible (KJV) unless otherwise noted.

Book Layout ©2013 BookDesignTemplates.com

Ordering Information:
Quantity sales. Special discounts are available on quantity purchases by corporations, associations, and others. For details, contact "Words N Wisdom" at the email address above.

Hold Tight to your Faith/ Nikki Crutchfield. —1st ed.
ISBN 978-0-6925935-0-9

Contents

This book is dedicated to God who is my Guide and constantly astounds me, my parents Toby and Violet Holmes support and encouragement personified, my sons, The OC Beach Bunnies, My Bishop Floyd E Nelson Jr. who said "Nikki don't just write a regular book!, and my amazing, fantabulous Husband, Mr. Brown Face!

"......my tongue is the pen of a ready writer".

—Psalms 45:1 (KJV)

Introduction

Believing in God, at times, can be difficult. Especially when we face insurmountable odds while in the back of our minds we think.... this has a strong possibility of not going in my favor. Why does this whisper of doubt enter our thoughts? Because some of us have lived long enough to know and maybe even experienced the following truism: *bad things will happen to good people.*

These unfortunate experiences can create a foggy barrier between skepticism and acts of faith with us standing on the side of the former. Christians with fogged vision miss the benefits of exercised faith.

It also prevents us from being steady overcomers when Satan attacks with distresses, distractions, and disappointments.

Furthermore, confidence in God that becomes snowed under an avalanche of unbelief, covers the positive and divine influence Christian Faith should have on those who are silently observing us.

This second book by Author Nikki Crutchfield is a compilation of "God reminds me" Christian Blogs. These blogs have been succinctly prepared as "reminders" that will encourage us to.......Hold Tight to our Faith!

[1]

Faith: A Matter of Survival

YEARS AGO, WHILE ON A FAMILY VACATION I ALMOST DROWNED. I was unaware that a riptide was occurring as I was busy jumping the waves. In the blink of an eye, I was swept out to where my feet could no longer touch the ocean floor. I am a strong, confident swimmer, as long as when I'm tired of swimming, there is something solid beneath my feet. As I alternated between floating, panicking, and drifting further out, a lifeguard eventually heard my cries for "HELP!" and came to save me. He had with him a hard, red, little, surf board like object.

It wasn't much, but grabbing hold to it, as he tugged me closer in to shore, readily calmed me down. Why? That board, despite its size, had substance.

Our faith is equivalent to that surf board. It is substantive despite how much of it you possess. The bible makes two declarative statements to support this. First

Hebrews 11:1 *"Now faith is the substance of things hoped for and the evidence of things not seen."*

In other words faith is the solid foundation of my hope and the tested proof of what I cannot tangibly see. Just the exhibition of faith communicates to God your confidence in Him. Here's the thing, you don't need much...just a little. A small amount of confidence can lead to a major impact. This leads us to the second declaration of the bible. Matthew 17:20 states:

"...if ye have faith as a grain of mustard seed, ye shall say unto this mountain, Remove hence to yonder place; and it shall remove; and nothing shall be impossible unto you." A grain of faith this small (.) makes the impossible possible!

In addition to doing major things, faith is connected to our Christian survival by serving to protect us.

If we look at Ephesians 6:10-18, it gives a detailed list of Christian Armor. When we get to verse 16 it states "Above all taking the shield of faith, wherewith ye shall be able to quench all the fiery darts of the wicked." What is Paul saying? Above all, or in addition to the other mentioned pieces of spiritual armor, take up faith. We are to be armed with confidence in God. He guarantees faith will protect us by quenching or extinguishing the fiery annoyances of life, sent to jeopardize our Christian belief. In layman terms: Faith will shut down the shenanigans of the enemy causing us to be triumphant against him!

The following three bible stories detail the *triumphant results* of possessing faith during times of testing, feelings of insecurity, and moments of adversity. All of which seek to hold us back or contradict the Power of God.

Up first:

Abraham's story of divine testing

After waiting 25 years for his promised son, Abraham is asked to present him as a whole burnt offering to God (Genesis 22). I am sure he is shaken to the core by the request, but he readily complies. Abraham shows uncommon faith for this uncommon situation: he is simultaneously obedient, while believing for an alternate outcome. That is multitasking at its best! We know that he had confidence in God when he informed his servants of the following *".....the lad and I will go yonder and worship and come again to you. (vs. 5)"* And again, when asked of his son about the missing sacrificial animal *"God will provide himself a lamb for a burnt offering…" (vs.8)*

God met Abraham's expectation and exceeded it.

Just as he is about to slay Isaac, his son, God calls out for Abraham to stop! He turns, and there caught in a small copse of shrubbery is a ram. If we remember, he predicts a *"lamb"*. However, the bible describes that a *"ram"* was *"caught in the thicket"*.

There is a significant difference between a lamb and a ram. A lamb is a young, weak male sheep that is normally under the watchful care of a shepherd, in the lowlands. While a ram is a strong, adult male sheep that roams the mountainside with a nomadic pack. What is equally important to note, is that, a ram has horns while a lamb does not. Making the ram a more adequate provision. I believe Abraham's statement of faith "God will provide himself a lamb for a burnt offering" released God to supernaturally meet his need.

Not only does crazy faith result in unusual provisions, but it allows us to be obedient to the commandments of God. Abraham's faithful obedience allowed him to see God revealed in a greater way. The moments when God is using what doesn't make sense to test our faith, quite possibly is Him positioning us for substance that exceeds our expectations. *Remember! The testing of our faith yields great rewards. Hoooooold on!*

Next is:

Moses, an early hero of the bible

He was the instrument God used to deliver His people from a 400 year old prison sentence. However, before being the deliverer, there were feelings of insecurity Moses had to conquer.

His feelings of insecurity included: low self-esteem "*Who am I*" (Exodus.3:11), how others would perceive him as a deliverer ""...*for they will say the Lord hath not appeared unto thee.*"(Ex. 4:1), and a physical impediment "*I am not eloquent*" (Ex. 5:10).

We, like Moses, use these realistic arguments to refute God's plan(s) for our life. The moment we embrace who we know we are and began to step out to be...insecurity pulls at our coattails freezing us in place. We then convince ourselves it's not meant for us to do.

Just like Moses, God is aware of what we lack *And yet*, He is still choosing us!

Let's take a moment, and contrast against these feelings of inadequacy by turning our attention to Psalms 139. This Psalm's is a meditative Psalm about God's omniscience. If we read Ps. 139:1-18

We see how David declares that God knows him....all of him, and that there is no part of David that God is surprised with. And even knowing that he was "*unperfect*" –rude and unformed matter- God still had "*precious thoughts towards him.*" Our faith, in God's choosing us, must far outweigh the thoughts, views, and opinions of others, as well as our own. We must keep in mind that we are uniquely wired by God and what we count as defective is just color to our characterization!

In the end, Moses's faith triumphed over his insecurities, causing millions of people to experience revolutionary change.

Choose to remember that your faith, as God's choice, will make a difference in the life of others!!

LASTLY WE HAVE:

The Hebrew boys

As they are commonly known, faced a serious and controversial situation (Daniel 3:12-27). The tenets of their faith strictly forbade the worshipping of a false image. Forced with a choice but unwilling to break the code of their belief, they chose death. Their unbreakable resolve raised a series of questions in my mind:

"How far am I willing to go to be faithful?

"Will I follow through with faith-filled decisions despite severe, adverse conditions?"

"Can I charge out into the storms of life, armed only with confidence in God....the outcome unknown?"

These valiant young men could answer all three with a resounding yes! They did not allow fear of the furnace to dampen their assurance in God. In fact, their faith took them into the fire, kept them while in the fire, and carried them back out again.

By the end of their story we read one interesting fact "the fire had no power". Faith will draw God into our situation, and He takes the heat out of the flame!

While our convictions may be challenged by situations that seemingly pose a threat to our physical bodies, we are to hold our righteous course. For there is no weapon, that the enemy can form, that will prosper against us!

Remember, adversity is going to come. It is our faith that empowers and strengthens us, and causes us to be triumphant in the end.

[2]

Faith requires Maintenance

THINK OF FAITH MAINTENANCE LIKE COURTING. During the courting phase of a relationship, all balances are carefully weighed. You are not too much of something or too little. You regard everything from the other person as important. There are minimal arguments, plenty of time spent together, attitudes remain at an all-time low, and all other suiters are cut off. *These careful actions are performed until the object of the one's desire is permanently held in their grasp.*

As believers, we must treat the hold on faith with the same tender regard. Because of its importance in obtaining what we need and desire in life, we must put forth required energy to guard our hold. This next chapter will delve into proper care, what happens if we neglect to care, and the benefits of properly caring for our handle on faith.

Many times I have struggled with what I can do as a believer and what I should avoid. In my late teens to early twenties I often debated should I "party". An invitation to celebrate with my cousin, at a local club, sparked such a debate. I insisted it wasn't the environment for me, but was convinced that I would be the life of the party (which incidentally I could be). I was equally convinced I didn't have to party should I come. So armed with the thought of "no participation required" I conceded, and lasted all of one hour. I could blame it on the beat of the go-go music coming out of the speakers, the laughter from the dance floor, the hottie who kept asking me "you sure you don't want to dance" or a combination of it all. Most likely....the combo. In any event, my convictions flew out the window like a caged bird finally set free. By the end of the night, I was totally absorbed into the club's environment, and didn't stop partying till the "last call" was made. That incident was my first real club experience, but it wouldn't be my last. I wandered in and out of the club/bar scene as a Christian, and it would be during these wanderings my faith was the weakest to non-existent.

I was walking a very dangerous line. Negotiating, about what is or is not permissible behavior as a believer is a time/energy waster. Here's our barometer: If we are expending strength holding onto pleasures that afford us little to no spiritual value/enhancement, while fighting against the pull of being completely absorbed into an alternative lifestyle..... That's a clear indication we should let it go. Newsflash! Now is not the time to waste energy.

It takes drive and attention to guard our hold on faith. If our energy and attention is diverted, our faith runs the risk of becoming *weak*. These person's become prime pickings for the enemy as Satan takes full advantage of our *weakened* state and introduces a challenge our faith is ill-equipped to handle. Consequently, we succumb and are defeated by the distresses, difficulties, or the distractions of life. Constant defeat will eventually lead to a falling away from the faith. When we fall away from the faith we publicly disgrace Christ. The one who suffered for our freedom from sin.

For the price He paid, a simple return on His investment would be for us to S E P A R A T E!

Separating is also a surefire way to attentively care for our faith. Let's take a look at the following verse:

> Numbers 6:2, states *"Speak unto the children of Israel, and say unto them, when either man or woman shall separate themselves to vow a vow of a Nazarite, to separate themselves unto the LORD:"*

Nazarites were a special type of people consecrated to God. Their consecration involved restrictions such as not drinking anything pertaining to the vine or grapes, no contact with dead bodies, nor could they cut their hair.   All of these limitations denoted their separation unto God.   The terms of conditions depended on how long the person decided to consecrate themselves. The vow could last 30, 60, 90 days or a lifetime. Some were born into this way of living: Samuel (1 Samuel 1:11) Samson (Judges 13:5). However, the people in this text did so of their own volition.   They voluntarily decided to separate themselves for dedicated service to God. Sidebar: God is worthy of our separating for service.

Let's translate how their restrictions can positively serve in guarding our grip on faith today. Nothing that could intoxicate was consumed.

I would consider casual drinking very risky behavior. It has the potential to draw us into a lifestyle we are not equipped to

successfully handle.

I did some digging and found out that there is now a demand to make wine stronger in flavor. This process involves leaving the grapes on the vine longer for stronger fermentation.

Which means there is a higher alcohol content. As we all know or should know… alcohol is a depressant. It is a drug that slows the central nervous system. Our central nervous system controls our mind and bodily functions.

Wait! There's more. The bible considers alcohol as a "strong drink", and should be avoided (Proverbs 23:29-33). Noah became drunk, and the bible says that his nakedness was uncovered by his son. Who then told, with pleasure, the delicate state of his father (Genesis 9:21, 22), undermining his godly authority.

In all, drinking is a distraction that dulls our minds and disables wise decision-making. *Clouded thoughts, cannot make sensible choices, based on biblical truth.* Alcohol consumption is an entry point for Satan to sneak in, and cause laxity in other areas. If we are not careful, we can find ourselves in situations less than ideal, like Noah, our character tarnished.

Nazarites were also forbidden to touch dead bodies. We will define dead as being, non-productive and un-Christ like individuals.   2 Corinthians 6:14-17 list several questions that I will drop right here for pondering:

14. "For what fellowship hath righteousness with unrighteousness? And what communion hath light with darkness?

15. "And what concord hath Christ with Belial? Or what part hath he that believeth with an infidel?"

16. "And what agreement hath a temple of God with idols?"

Verse 16 is where the questions stop. We see that we are strongly being instructed against any type of:

"fellowship", "communion" "concord", "part", or "agreement" .

with anyone who we know is not committed to God. Intimate involvement with those who have no intention of living for Him, will influence negative behavior.

Verse 17 then follows with this advice:

"Wherefore come out from among them and be ye SEPARATE, saith the Lord...."

Successful faith holders, are marked off from un-Christ-like individuals, by boundaries!

Lastly, they were forbidden to cut their hair. The hair growth was considered a crown and a visible way to mark them as being different. An outward display of an inner conviction will let others know;

"I'm unlike you. My conversation, my attitude, and my general way of living is different from yours."

When we faithfully follow Godly behavior it should strengthen us. Why? Godly behavior fuels our inner connection to God, and it is our inner connection to God, that empowers us (Romans 8:13).

These are vital points within the act of separating ourselves as believers. Should we choose to ignore the responsibility of guarding our faith by these means, we can find ourselves out in the cold like Samson.

There is a cost to not separating.

More than once, while separating laundry items, some of my whites got mixed in with my colored. The results were disastrous. Cute white pants and tops were ruined and ultimately thrown out because the dye from the colored clothing bled into the fabric.

Ruinous results are certain for a believer, who makes the mistake of intermingling or intermixing their lives with unbelievers. Such was the case with Samson.

To be honest, I have mixed emotions about the life of Samson (Judges 13-16). He judged Israel for 20 years, and did amazing feats, but his existence was plagued with improper decisions that ultimately cost him his life. Who walks with God for 20 years and ends up being duped, by one, Delilah?

While the bible does not tell us what Samson's 20 years looked like, as he judged, it does give us a peek into who he is, through his early decisions. Some of which went directly against his Nazarite vows.

Although not a Nazarite rule, but definitely an expectation as an Israelite, He intermarried though it was strictly forbidden (Deut. 7:3). When that relationship failed, he pursued prostitutes. Samson also touched a non-living thing, the carcass of an animal. The touching of the dead was a strictly prohibited Nazarite rule.

It's potentially clear, Samson was lacking in his convictions.

These behavioral contradictions may have been the reason he easily entertained the wrong person, who would set him up for abject failure. When she asked Samson after his strength, his dallying with Delilah eventually violated another Nazarite prohibition, the cutting of his hair. When his hair was cut, it symbolized his connection with God being severed. Now at the mercy of his enemy, weak and defenseless, disastrous results were inevitable. Samson's eyes were gouged out by fire. He was made to be a court jester for his adversary, and reduced to grinding grain in a prison as a slave. Ultimately, though God allows him to be "avenged of his two eyes" his life is sacrificed in the process.

Could it be that Samson's supernatural use lulled him into a false sense of security?

To be sure, a false sense of security will set in when we are used in spite of poor choices. While it may appear as if we are getting away with making careless decisions, when we least expect it, like Samson, we will look for the strength needed to defeat the enemy, and it will not be there.

When I read his story, I'm reminded of how quickly God slaps my hand the moment I get out of line! At first this divine reaction seems unfair, until I took a closer at Samson's ramifications. I realized, there is no way I would want to trade places with him. I do not want to be one, where God utilizes me "in spite of" my propensities.

God was looking to defeat Israel's enemy. Samson's predilection's would not stop or hinder that divine goal. Rather, God used Samson in spite of his wayward tendencies. How do I state this authoritatively? The bible declares in 2 Timothy 2:19, 20:

"Nevertheless the foundation of God standeth sure, having this seal, The Lord knoweth them that are his. And let everyone that nameth the name of Christ depart from iniquity. 20 "But in a great house there are not only vessels of gold and of silver, but also of wood and of earth; and some to honor and some to dishonor."

What is Paul intimating? In the house of God are persons who are considered honorable and dishonorable vessels- *chosen instruments.* What sets the two types apart is found in verse 21"

"If a man purge himself from these; he shall be a vessel unto honour, sanctified, and meet for the master's use, and prepared unto every good work."

This may be tough to accept, but God *will* still use those strong-willed in their behavior, to accomplish a divine end.

Matthew 7::22, 23 "Many will say to me in that day, Lord, Lord, have we not prophesied in thy name? and in thy name cast out devils? And in thy name done many wonderful works? 23 "And then will I profess unto them, I never knew you; depart from me, ye that work iniquity."

Workers of iniquity are those who honor God with their lips and perform religious duties, but their heart is far from Him. They do not endeavor to live up to God's desired standards, sinning without hesitation.

I do not take the liberty of putting Samson into hell with mentioning Matthew 7:22, 23 as I neither judge nor jury. What I am pointing out, is that, failure to separate ourselves from ungodly people and pursuits puts us in unexpected and precarious situations. If Samson had lived differently, could his outcome been different? I would say yes.

Now we will balance out the negative with the positive:

There is another judge, who shows us the benefits of being separate.

A Confluence is a phenomenal sight to behold. There are two bodies of water with distinct colors that meet, while in some cases the colors stay distinctive. This clear dissimilarity is what every believer should be striving towards. Where we are able to encounter people throughout life and not lose our clarity as Christians.

I know, without question, that we will have to interact with people not of our same conviction. However, what's important to remember is to refrain from intermingling or becoming intertwined with them.

The following is a powerful testimony of a young boy by the name of Samuel (1 Samuel 2) who maintained his clarity as a faithful believer while in the midst of a faithless group of people. He is the son of Elkanah and Hannah who was "asked of" by God. In return for blessing Hannah with the child, she promised him back for temple service. In short, Samuel's life is pledged as a Nazarite at birth. When he is weaned at the age of 3, Hannah returns to the temple and leaves him in the care of Eli the priest, to minister before the Lord.

The conditions in which he grows up are deplorable. Everyone was doing what was right in their own eyes. This contemptible attitude towards God did not escape the confines of the temple. Of which Eli's natural sons (Hophni and Phineas) were the biggest perpetrators.

However, despite their scandalous and corrupt behavior as described in 1 Samuel 2:17 we find in the very next verse (18) these words recorded about Samuel:

"But Samuel ministered before the Lord, being a child, girded with a linen ephod."

As a young child, he makes a conscious choice to be dissimilar from the sinful nature he is surrounded by. This decision leads to *benefits of being separate.*

The benefits of being separate are found in:

1 Samuel 3:19, 20 "And Samuel grew and the Lord was with him, and he did not let none of his words fall to the ground."

"And all of Israel from Dan even to Beer-sheba knew that Samuel was established to be a prophet of Lord."

The bible declared that the Word of God was "precious" or very rare in those days, and there was no open vision. This meant God rarely spoke, and there was no one to communicate the will of God until…. Samuel's arrival on the scene. Can we let that sink in for a while? Samuel became the starting point for spiritual revitalization!

As a result of his separatist lifestyle, God was favorably with him. He 'grew" or matured into greatness and the ministry assigned to his hands, was both effective and efficient to those around him.

Remember! Guarding your hold on faith may require effort, but it is beneficial.

Be S E P A R A T E!

As we enter the next few sections, we are going to see the evidence of faith holders. When you tightly hold to your confidence in God… that looks like something. Let's find out what?

[3]

Faith Excludes

FAITHFULLY FOLLOWING GOD AGAINST THE ODDS, will appear foolish to the outside world.

Because of this, the exhibition of faith will sometimes cause us to exclude people from knowing the full intent of our faith-filled movements.

In 2 Kings chapter 4 there is a widow, her sons, a prophet…. and a door?

A widow has come to the prophet Elisha because she is in dire straits. Her creditors are looking to make her two son's indentured servants in order to pay off her debt. Elisha then asks what she had in the house, by way of appeasing her creditors. Her response was a pot or a flask of oil. After hearing what she had, he instructs for her and her sons to go and borrow as many vessels as they could from her neighbors. When she returned, Elisha gave her two other directives. He told her in Verse 4—

"To shut the door with only her and her sons in the house, then to pour out the little oil that she had into the larger vessels."

Why must she and her family seclude themselves away from the world before following his instructions? I choose to believe, that while performing this extreme act of faith, any would-be criticism or disbelief was to be preemptively excluded!

Let's imagine that some of her neighbors were speculative of why she was borrowing vessels. Let's further picture they decided to show up at her house, uninvited, and saw what she was doing; pouring out oil from her small flask into the larger pots. Chances are, they would have either voiced their doubt or outright called her crazy.

Crazy faith may attract potential doubters, but I give you license to shut the door, right in their face, and hold tight to your FAITH. Do what doesn't make sense!

Remember! Faith may at times, require

Exclusion!

[4]

Faith Responds with Praise

PRAISE IS AN ACT OF FAITH. We lift our hands, dance, and send up shouts of Hallelujah to a God that we have never seen. Nevertheless, faith says that He hears us and relishes our acts of adoration. Not only is praise and worship a way to show our esteem, it is the appropriate response to constricting, and rest-stealing situations.

I have had some experiences, in life, that have overwhelmed my mind. Situations that have caused me sleepless nights. My thoughts would be running a mile a minute, playing through all types of "what if" scenarios.

"What if" I had done that, or "what if" I had responded that way, or made that decision?"

I am not alone.

Besides the "what if" game we play late into the night, we:

Late night troll through Facebook or Instagram (liking statues/pics @ 2:32am)

Late night eat, and/or

Late night shop (QVC style)

What I was doing, and what many of us do, is we allow overwhelming situations to rob us of our peace and try to remedy that insomnia with methods that do not cure our ails.

PEACE ISN'T ACHIEVED THROUGH POINTLESS PURSUITS.

When challenges regulate the direction of our thoughts during a time when we should be asleep, there is a biblical alternative that will simultaneously calm and free us.

The bible tells the story in (Acts 16:16-40) of two men by the name of Paul and Silas. Specifically, they were the instruments used in the spiritual deliverance of a young woman. This young woman, a soothsayer of sorts, made important men a lot of money. So upset were these men on losing their moneymaker that they had Paul and Silas beaten, then jailed. Additionally, they were led to the inner section of the prison, shackled to a wooden beam, and kept under the watchful eye of the prison guard.

In the middle of their imprisonment the bible records in Acts 16:25-27 the following —

"And at midnight Paul and Silas prayed, and sang praises unto God: and the prisoners heard them."

"And suddenly there was a great earthquake, so that the foundations of the prison were shaken: and immediately all the doors were opened, and every one's bands were loosed." Verse 27 begins with *"And the keeper of the prison awaking out of his sleep...."*

As I read these verses there was something that caught my attention. Why were Paul and Silas awake at midnight? Additionally, why were the rest of the prisoners either not asleep or their rest, easily disturbed? In comparison to their jailor, who was in close proximity, and was in such a deep slumber that it took an earthquake to awaken him.

Was it possible that the situation they were all in caused them some distress? Distress that induced restlessness and made room for runaway thoughts of; "What if's?"

Or distress that caused fitful rest? Sleep, that is easily broken or disturbed.

Whatever the case, we see Paul and Silas finally use their faith to properly respond to their misery. *"They prayed and sang praises."* When they sang praises, it meant that they were singing the scriptures or Paschal Hymns. The Paschal Hymns included chapters in the book of Psalms. Directly, they were singing Psalms 113-118. Here's what some of their lyrics looked like:

Psalms 113:7 "He raiseth up the poor out of the dust, and lifteth the needy out of the dunghill."

Psalms 114:2 "Judah is his sanctuary, and Israel is his dominion."

Psalms 115:18 "But we will bless the Lord from this time forth and forevermore. Praise the Lord."

Psalms 116:16 "....thou hast loosed my bonds."

Psalms 117:2a "For his merciful kindness is great toward us...."

Psalms 118:17 "I shall not die, but live, and declare the works of the Lord."

.

Creating an atmosphere where God dwells is better than any other prescribed method of easing a troubled mind. When He tangibly settles into our presence, all other white noise has to cease. Right then, all the tempestuous thoughts stop.

After the excitement, that comes with praising and worshiping our God, peace and relaxation follows.

Paul and Silas used part of their restless energy for praise and worship. This allowed them to focus on the God of their salvation. They received a divine reaction (a stir of excitement) causing their bands to be "loosed". The word "loosed," in the Greek, is defined as to be loosened, relaxed or calmed. Can I insert a little tidbit for free? It wasn't just their bands loosed…but "everyone's bands were loosed" If you change your method in dealing with distressful situations, it could cause a chain reaction. That someone else, those right in our personal space, might find freedom and peace without resorting to alternative methods that don't profit.

Once the earthquake ended and they were freed, peace and relaxation ensued (Acts 16:27-40).

Remember! The evidence of faith held tightly in our grasp, occurs when we respond to troubling situations with Praise.

[5]

Faith Endures

"*ASK, AND IT SHALL BE GIVEN YOU; seek, and ye shall find, knock, and it shall be opened unto you: For everyone that asketh receiveth; and he that seeketh findeth; and to him that knocketh it shall be opened.*" These are the words of Christ spoken in Matthew 7:7, 8. These instructions are easy and looks to have immediate results. And while this is true at times, there are moments when what we ask for is slow in coming. Where, for some of us, we are still looking for/expecting what has yet to manifest. Do we get impatient or tired of waiting on God?

I have a very impatient nature and I do not wait well, but I am working on it....by degrees. Sidebar: isn't it just like us to be patient when we need to change somethings about ourselves, but we desire everything else to happen in an instant!

When I was a young girl, my younger brother and I were sent to the corner store. We were standing at the light waiting for it to turn green. I became intolerant of the wait, looked to my left and right, took my little brother's hand and stepped out into the street. Bam! We were hit by a car. I was hospitalized for up to two months. After which, I was sent home in a body cast for the rest of my recuperative period. At the time of the accident, I was in the second grade. When I returned to school, I was a third grader.

My impatience hurt me, and caused me to miss out on key points for my development as a student. As well as putting someone I love in danger. Impatience will hurt our chances in obtaining what we need from God. We can move in our own esteem and damage the situation much like Abraham and Sarah did (Genesis 16). Or miss out altogether like Saul (1 Samuel 13). Please keep the following in mind as it relates to petitioning God:

HIS RESPONSE TIME IS TOTALLY UP TO HIM.

With that said…Do we lessen our grip on faith and stop asking/believing? No.

The important factor of faith is the boldness to ask and to keep asking, if necessary. Why? Because a defeatist attitude quits inquiring, when a positive outcome looks unlikely. Please keep in mind that God knows how to communicate an unequivocal no. And unless He has told you no…keep asking.

The woman in the following texts, Mark 7:24-30 and Matthew 15:21-28 shows us that patient tenacity, along with constantly asking, gets it done! The accounts go a little like this:

Jesus had just traveled, by foot, 50 miles to seek solitude in the coast of Tyre and Sidon, a gentile city "and would have no man to know it" Mk. 7:24. We don't know if knowledge of Jesus being in her town gave the woman pause, as the Jews had no dealings with the gentiles at this time. But when she "heard" he was there, she took her opportunity to ask him for what she needed. Matthew's account states that after her initial request, she is blatantly ignored. She keeps asking frustrating the disciples who want Jesus to *"send her away"*. Instead of sending her away, he continues to delay her request, to which she responds with worship! Followed by a plea of *"Lord help me."* She is then publicly humiliated and called a *"dog"* Whew! Does she call it quits at this point? No. She doesn't even appear to be offended or out of patience with Jesus attitude towards her.

She decided what she needed was worth more than suffering a bruised ego, an attempted dismissal, or being snubbed.

In the end her humble reply:

"Truth, Lord: yet the dogs eat of the crumbs which fall from their masters' table" caused Jesus to answer her dogged faith!

Motivated Jesus to reply with:

"For this saying go thy way; the devil is gone out of thy daughter."

This woman's faith endured and she received what she needed.

Remember! Confidently asking, repeatedly when necessary, is a sign that faith is held firmly in your hand!

[6]

Faith is Responsible

EXHIBITION OF FAITH CAN BE CONNECTED TO FOLLOWING DIVINE OBLIGATIONS. What are these responsibilities?

We are assigned specific gifting's, and are held accountable to act upon them. Failure to do so disappoints God.

It's just like the expectation a parent has for their child or children. Parents will assign household duties based on capabilities. We have faith that our kids can do what we have asked. So we are disappointed and angry when we arrive home, or check on their progress, and our expectations have not been met. In our minds, it's not that they didn't understand what to do, or how to perform the task, they simply choose not to do it. As a result, negative consequences occur.

FAILURE TO ACT IS FAILURE TO BE OBEDIENT.

As we said earlier, God assigns to us gifts. He has faith in His children and is confident that we are capable of carrying out what He has gifted us to be. It would then seem fair that God is disappointed and upset, and holds us liable for the lack of use. It's true He is the dominating force within us, but there is some responsibility on our part. There are practical actions of faith that we should be initiating towards using our gifts.

Matthew 25:14-30 conveys a parable of accountability. The story begins with a man who has dispersed his valuable possessions to three men. But he does not do so haphazardly. Matthew 25:15 states that he gave;

"to every man according to his several abilities."

So to one he gave five talents, to another two, and to the last, one. Only two step forward and act responsibly. They knew the expectations of the master, and what to do with their talents, and did what they were capable of doing. But the last man, who also knew the expectation of his master, knew what he is supposed to do with his talent, consciously decides so bury it....beneath the dirt.

When the master returned, each of the servants give an account. The first two doubled their efforts. But as the last one, who didn't rise to the occasion, concludes his reasoning for burying his talent…under the dirt, the story takes a dark turn.

Jesus called this servant;

"wicked" "slothful" and "unprofitable."

In other words, he correlates him to a lazy derelict that was useless. In addition, the man is forced to watch his talent stripped away and given to someone else.

Ultimately, he is cast into outer darkness (Hell) where he will be exposed to "weeping" and "gnashing of teeth".

I ASKED MYSELF, DID THE PUNISHMENT MEET THE CRIME IN JESUS PARABLE? THE ANSWER IS AN UNQUESTIONABLE YES!

2 Corinthians 4:7 (paraphrased) states *"we have treasure in earthen vessels" (earthen vessels being us, comprised of dirt).* While our gifting's are held inside of us, they shouldn't be buried down deep, and ill-used under the "dirt". Burying our talent or refusal to let it surface is a direct act of disobedience.

Please note: Fear and anxiety are not valid reasons for inactivity. There is something bigger than our unease at risk. *Sinners are dying while we are digging…hiding our talents.*

This parable, a part of the Olivet Discourse, was delivered right before Jesus began his journey to the cross. He knew he would be leaving his disciples soon, and that they would now be responsible for continuing the work that He started.

TODAY, AS WELL AS THEN, THIS PARABLE CONVEYS THE IMPORTANCE OF FAITHFUL SERVICE TO THE KINGDOM OF GOD. IT IS OUR RESPONSIBILITY, AS FAITHFUL BELIEVERS, TO CONTINUE BUILDING ON THE WORK OF JESUS CHRIST. POSITIVELY IMPACTING THE WORLD FOR HIM UNTIL HE RETURNS.

Remember! Our Faith acts responsibly when we utilize our gifts for the Kingdom

[7]

Faith's Approach and Acceptance is Graceful

WHEN WE ARE HELD IN AN UNDESIRABLE CONDITION, WE HAVE TWO RECOURSES: we can either complain about what is going on, or graciously deal with the matter until change occurs. I believe, at times, we can become frustrated and contentious when it's unclear why God allows certain situations to occur, in addition to us being forced to deal with its discomfort.

Some years ago I experienced a devastating and unfair circumstance. The death of my younger brother Tony. He was killed while in a correctional detention center. They attempted to convince us that his death was a suicide. Here's my major concern with that scenario: he was scheduled to come home 2 weeks prior to his death, and was only detained for violation of his probation. A simple misdemeanor charge of trespassing (hanging out in the wrong neighborhood). Which raised the pondering thought... *that is something to kill yourself over?* Later, the truth would emerge. His life was TAKEN by someone in authority. The weeks following his death were filled with disbelief, grief and finally anger. This anger covered me like a shroud. I was angry at God for allowing it to happen. I remember asking Him **WHY!!** And it wasn't in a gentle tone it was like "why you didn't do something about it!" "Why didn't you prevent it from happening?!!! Why weren't the ones responsible....held responsible?!! For weeks I walked around with this internal chip on my shoulder until one night, I attended a church service.

At the conclusion of the guest preacher's message she called a prayer line. Then she gave me this intense look (some of you know what I mean), and called me forward. Her next words sent me into absolute shock. She said "God said don't ask Him Why? Accept what He allows." Yes, I crumpled like a weightless napkin. Mainly because God proved that He heard my private complaint. Side bar: He is listening and is mindful of us.

Moving forward from that statement, one would think it to mean that I was never to question God when I didn't understand why some situations took place, and I was forced to ride out the discomfort.

If this is true, how could Jesus be overheard asking "why hast thou forsaken me?" A question Christ directed to God, as he was suffering on the cross. So is it *that* we ask or *how* we ask? I tend to think it is the latter.

While I am a firm proponent of 'because I said so" as a direct reply to my children's inquiries, there are moments when they are truly perplexed about our parental decisions and it is during those times we permit them to "question us". We have taught them *how* to approach us, which assists with keeping our hands at our sides. There won't be contention *begetting* contention.

What am I saying?

There is a difference between striving with God and inquiring.

Isaiah 45:9 states *"Woe unto him that striveth* (contend) *with his Maker.* While in Isaiah 45:11 it reads: *"Ask me of things to come concerning my sons and concerning the works of my hands command ye me."* Why is the prophet Isaiah relaying these words to the children of Israel?

They, like us, would eventually find themselves in a fixed situation that was not going to amend. God's people would face involuntary exile and would have a tough time adjusting to this uncomfortable situation. In anticipation of them taking issue with His decisions, forced exile and a non-Jew deliverer, God patiently guides them. These two verses teach the following: instead of approaching Him in a contentious manner that results in reproof, they are to humbly inquire about the prophetic word He spoke over their condition and to direct His power on their behalf.

Here's what's so powerful about those statements:

1. A reminder of God's promises during a difficult and prolonged circumstance is the shining light at the end of a very long and dark tunnel.

Today, the justice surrounding Tony's death remains unanswered for. And I graciously ask God about these failed attempts of justice and recently His word of encouragement to me was- "*I have already done what I promised, time just has to catch up to manifestation.*" *Can you imagine what hope and ease of tension that gave me?!* I feel the gap between my brother's death and justice closing!

2. When our faith accepts what God allows and we graciously inquire about our situation(s) He grants us access to His power.

Quickly, let's get back to the children of Israel. When God tells them to "*command the works of His hands*" it's a no-brainer about where *I* would direct His power.... change our situation now and free us..... Please and thank you☺.

But their timeframe was still not to be modified. Then the question becomes how would His power be beneficial to them, while their situation remained unchanged?

God tells them in (Jeremiah 29:5-7) to build them a life while in captivity. As they built these new lives, He told them to pray for peace. If they didn't know what to *command God to do*, His power could be utilized for creating harmony in their current situation, until their situation reflected their word of deliverance. Sometimes, as much as I would like a particular situation to adjust to my liking...If God grants me peace that "passeth all understanding", peace that keeps my heart and mind-*my thoughts and emotions under control*, it's enough for me!

The moments in life, where you are forced to tough it out- your faith and implicit trust in God should encourage a courteous approach to Him and acceptance of what is your current lot. In return, you can expect a reminder of His promises concerning you. You can expect tranquility- the power of His peace to cover you- until your situation turns into your moment of freedom and/or redemption.

Remember! People of faith won't contend with God's sovereignty.

Our time together is coming to a close. I am actually quite sad to see this book end. In some way, I have imagined us having a strong dialogue about our faith in God. However, before I say goodbye, I want to leave this last encouraging message:

When we find our faith alternately being chipped away by doubt, and are exhausted....tired of fighting with the trials, temptations, and tribulations of life. We can cry out like the helpless father in Mark 9:24, who said:

"Lord I believe, help thou mine unbelief"

The final chapter of this book will detail the provision God has made to support us in times where unbelief battles ferociously against our faith. This provision comes by way of……..

[8]

The Good Shepherd

Spotters play a major safety role in weightlifting. They spot persons who are lifting heavy weights repetitiously. When the weight-lifter starts to struggle or becomes stuck and can't lift the bar back up, they don't have to let go. The person spotting them, who has been carefully watching, steps in to add strength.

In life, we can encounter weighty distresses, discouragements, and difficulties. However, we do not have to succumb to unbelief. When the weight of any of these becomes too much, we have the world's best Spotter. He is a Shepherd (John 10:11) who constantly watches over us and adds to us strength. With this added power we can manage the heaviness, and hold tight to our faith at the same time.

Let's look into this role of a Shepherd who spots us:

There are some jobs that are considered menial. Menial occupations are often overlooked, and undervalued. Not long ago, I was in desperate need of employment and being choosy was not an option. So with my husband's words reverberating through my mind, "anything beats a blank", I took a job less in responsibility and pay. I went from being a manager to a catering assistant. To say the least, this reversal of roles was a shock to my sensibilities and made adjusting uncomfortable. Despite the difficulty of the transition, I quickly learned that menial did not mean meaningless. My contribution played a major role in that Law firm. The quality customer service I provided enhanced every client's experience.

Although this transition is minute in comparison, Our Lord and Savior Jesus Christ made a similar adjustment. He left a prominent position in Heaven, and as mentioned in John 10:11, He took on the menial role of a "spiritual" Shepherd. During that time, the job of a shepherd was the lowest form of employment and hugely snubbed. Yet, Jesus proudly associates Himself with this title. In taking on this role, it positioned Him low enough to reach us, enhancing our lives by introducing us to a right relationship with God. Jesus is "the good shepherd [who] giveth his life for the sheep".

Beyond sacrificing His life, our Shepherd continues to spot us. He ensures that we do not buckle in defeat, under the weight of life, and ultimately let go of our faith. Psalms 23 gives us the ways in which our *"Good Shepherd"* stands watch over us waiting to help us in the time of need:

"The Lord is my Shepherd; I shall not want." (Psalms 23:1)

Although it may seem our concerns are overlooked by the watching Shepherd, they are not. The bible declares in (Luke 12:7) that the very hairs on our head are numbered-(Greek) *to be counted*. Meaning (and I'm borrowing the following phrase) "if hair follicle number 286 falls out, God knows!" A God that conscientious is surely concerned about our weightier needs. Should we take inventory of our lives, we will find that He has always taken care of us. And if He is the same yesterday, today, and forever...... then most assuredly, we can count on Him just as David did.

The Psalmist David states the above verse with a sense of determination. He is absolutely sure that God will, and desires to take care of him as a Shepherd might tend to his sheep. Some believe that David wrote this Psalms in his adult years, and that Psalms 23 is a reflection of his life. His confidence of God's care can be derived from his past experience of God's deliverance.

Not only does our past deliverances give us hope, but the term Shepherd is defined as one "who entreats a friend."

A friend is considered a companion. Friends know one another intimately. They are able to read moods and emotions clearly, and respond accordingly. A good friend is invaluable. While I value the physical compassion afforded through close friendships, there is no friend like God. What sets Him apart is His readiness to hear from us, even when our concerns are the same as they were the day before. He is not restricted to time, so it is never too late to reach out to him (I'm talking like 2am! He is alert and ready to listen and answer us). He knows us intimately and despite the millions of those who call on Him for what they need, He accurately responds to individual requests. What I find most important about having God as a friend is this….He holds us down- *translation*- He keeps our secret….secret!

I believe that David found and appreciated the value of a divine friendship. Yes, he had Jonathan his best friend, but when he was killed we never hear of another, in David's life, to that degree. What we do know is that he pours his heart out, through his writings, as though speaking to a close friend. Psalms 61 is a testament to this fact.

The Psalmist sets a pattern we can follow to encourage extreme confidence in God. That our past experiences, coupled with a divine relationship ensures the Shepherd will spot us the assistance we need. Here is something else to consider: Even when the person benching the weight does not call out for help, the spotter can sense the struggle. He senses that person's silent communication for assistance.

Our Shepherd is the same. We may not be able to utter that cry for help, but because *"his eye is on the sparrow...."* He sees our struggle and steps in.

Remember The Good Shepherd supports us thru
Care and consistency

"He maketh me to lie down in green pastures" *then* "He leadeth me beside the still waters" (Psalms 23:2)

The world's current climate is both tumultuous and chaotic. Reading or watching the news, while informative, can be very depressing. If we add in our personal tests and trials.......well we got us a right crazy mix.... *An atmospheric pressure that challenges our hold on faith!*

But. There. Is. Hope!

This verse promotes peace through reading God's word, and times of refreshing from being in his presence. Psalms 56:10 states *"In God will I praise his word: in the Lord will I praise his word."* Both scriptures, Ps. 56:10 and 23:2, are prayers of trust for deliverance. He writes Psalms 56 during very turbulent times. David has killed Goliath which makes him a hero to the people, but a menace in the eyes of King Saul. Overcome with jealousy, Saul makes every attempt to end David's life. For this reason, David goes on the run and has to find refuge in the camp of the Philistines, his sworn enemy. While seeking asylum amongst his enemies, he feigns himself insane in order to survive.

Can you imagine the stress of David's environment? He's running from a killer, he is living with his adversary, and having to pretend that he is crazy. However, he does not let go of his faith! It is evidenced with these verses, that David has learned he can find peace, *and we can find peace*, in an atmosphere filled with worship, and recitation of God's word! Despite this time of despair, through peace he held onto his faith in God.

Remember! God uses our quality time with Him to support our hold on Faith!

"HE RESTORETH MY SOUL......"
(PSALM 23:3A)

I have always been an avid Praiser. I believe the song "When I think of his goodness and all he has done for me, I can dance....." was written for and about me. Then one day, many years ago, I experienced the embarrassing consequence of a poor decision. While my delicate situation blossomed, I believed myself to be the subject of side-eyes and whispered conversations. Self-condemnation and my heightened sensibilities, caused me to grow deathly silent in the one place I found the most joy, church. Yes, I had asked God to forgive me, but the problem was me forgiving myself and moving forward. For a short while I let go of my faith, unable to believe that I was truly forgiven. It would take eight months to slowly roll pass, before my faith resurfaced and allowed me to resume my life as a Praiser.

It was during the middle of praise and worship that a woman, whom we will call "Hercules" came and whispered life-changing words in my ear....

"God said you are back in right standing with Him"

That one sentence, was filled with words that restored or refreshed my faith I was confident once again. I believed, God wanted to hear me give Him shouts of praise in His house, and well.....I tore that bench up!

When the Psalmist stated that God *"restores his soul"* It is possible that David lost a little of who he was or was out of character. Could it be that his experience(s) veiled his consistent disposition under sadness or depression? Whatever the case, David declares himself brought back to his original state, through divine revitalization!

Like David, we can lose a bit of our nature when encountering difficulties! Our regular disposition can be overshadowed with gloom, hiding who we naturally are. But also like David, God will restore us- bring back the activity of our true personality.

IT IS IMPORTANT TO NOTE THAT ACHIEVING THIS TYPE OF RESTORATION CAN BE FOUND IN THE EXAMPLE I SHARED, GOD'S WORD PROPHETICALLY SPOKEN. HOWEVER, WHEN NO ONE IS NEAR TO WHISPER TO US WORDS OF COMFORT, THAT IN NO WAY HINDERS THE RESTORATIVE POWER OF GOD. HE WILL CAUSE US TO HEAR A TIMELY WORD PREACHED, READ, AND/OR SUNG THAT WILL LIFT OUR HEARTS AND MINDS, TIGHTENING OUR GRIP ON FAITH IN HIM.

"...HE LEADETH ME IN THE PATHS OF RIGHTEOUSNESS FOR HIS NAME'S SAKE." (PSALMS 23:3B)

Most times, scratch that, ALL the time a Christian's life is under a microscope, and we are held to a higher standard. With that said, kindly note the following: Someone. Is. Always. Watching. (Please see the cover of this book) And here is the kicker.....in most cases, you are not aware you are being watched....and judged!

This may seem unfair, but the moment we accepted Jesus Christ into our life, started making changes, and professing our salvation, we signed up to be silently observed. As the salt of the earth and the light of the world (Matthew 5: 13, 14). "We may be the only Jesus that people see".

But let's take a moment and look at it from a different, more positive perspective.

Millions of Americans claim Christianity, yet there are those who do not. Further still, are persons who are not stable in their faith. Collectively these individuals do not share our passion for the One and True living God.

The second portion of Psalms 23:3b reads:

"he leadeth me in the paths of righteousness for his names sake."

What does this mean? That He can guide our movements, we are the better for it and we make Him look good while visibly obeying His commands. So imagine for a moment, those around us make a pivotal decision to join the Christian Faith, or become stronger in their convictions just by observing our obedience to God. The bible also declares in the latter portion of Psalms 84:11:

"no good thing will he withhold from them that walk uprightly".

Making this a win-win-win! God is exalted in the earth, people are turning fully to Him, and our righteous living advances good things towards us!

Remember! The Good Shepherd will guide us to goodness, Hold tight to your faith……. It has rewards.

"YEA THOUGH I WALK THROUGH THE VALLEY OF THE SHADOW OF DEATH, I WILL FEAR NO EVIL: FOR THOU ART WITH ME: THY ROD AND THY STAFF THEY COMFORT ME." (PSALMS 23:4)

Sheep are naturally defenseless animals. While they can sense when danger is near, they are not equipped to outrun, outmaneuver, and are simply outmatched by their predator.

Very often, we like sheep, can sense impending danger. We can experience predatory situations that we cannot outrun, outmaneuver, and are simply outmatched for. We are not alone.

Psalms 23:4 is a dark expression of a terrifying moment in David's life. He may have been considered outmatched and unable to outrun, or outmaneuver his opponent, but he does not fear.

What hope did David have? He writes:

"Yea, though I walk through the valley of the shadow of death, I will fear no evil: for thou art with me; thy rod and thy staff they comfort me."

He derived comfort from knowing, he is not left alone to face his terrifying circumstance. That God's presence is with him during these times, and in His hands are the symbolic representations of a rod and a staff. The rod speaks to His ability to fight for David, while the staff provides concrete support. This in turns gives him comfort- the ability to sigh with relief.

Today, nothing we face should cause us to feel helplessly cornered with fear, nullifying our faith and trust in God. We may be outmatched, and are unable to outrun or outmaneuver our enemy, but we have this assured relief. God is a Shepherd that will fight for and support His people! Read 2 Chronicles 20:17.

Remember! God defends of the defenseless!

"THOU PREPAREST A TABLE BEFORE ME IN THE PRESENCE OF MINE ENEMIES..." (PSALMS 23:5)

The story of "Cinderella" is a timeless classic. It is the tale of a young girl whose "haters", were people close to her. Though reduced to being her haters' servant, she does so with a smile.

Cinderella is content with her life and takes nothing special for herself. But a moment arises, and she wants to attend a ball held in honor of the prince. She is promised that she can go as long as she gets her work done. While keeping up with her chores, Cinderella and her friends, the mice and birds, work feverishly to make a dress. They work in anticipation of her being able to attend the dance, and they do it.

As her step-mother and step-sisters are leaving for the evening's festivities, thinking with certainty that Cinderella is not going, she calls out for them to "wait" as she quickly descends the stairs.

They watch her approach, envious with how pretty she is. As she draws near, her step-sisters attack her and rip her gown to shreds. Distraught and broken, Cinderella tearfully runs outside. But as we know the story doesn't end there. She received a visit from her fairy god-mother who transformed her into a vision of beauty, enabling her to attend the ball. The whole while she is there, she doesn't make an attempt to alert her family of her presence. Cinderella is enjoying favor, but undercover.

She knows she has to leave by midnight or risk being discovered. However, Cinderella is so caught up with the prince, time sneaks up on her. As she hears the sound of the bell tolling midnight, she flees, leaving behind one....glass....slipper.

The next day she never mentions her attendance at the ball, keeping her moment of favor a pleasurable secret. Soon though, Ole Cindy has to make a life-altering decision...the Prince is looking for the girl who fits the glass slipper in order to marry her. Does she reveal she is the one who left the shoe behind or does she keep silent?

While she is digesting the news of her life potentially changing forever, the prince is traveling the countryside with no success. No one can fit the glass slipper.

Sidebar- what God has for you, it is for you!

Finally he reaches Cinderella's house. The stepmother suspects, but isn't sure that Cinderella is the girl until....She sees her running down the steps, after having escaped the room she locked her in, and notices her feet are small enough to fit the glass slipper.

She first tried to block her by stating she was a lowly servant who in no way could have been at the ball. But the King's guards, sent to assist the prince, would make certain that every fair maiden had their turn. Now desperate, the evil step-mother is determined to stop this pivotal moment from happening for Cinderella, and she engineers for the glass slipper to fall and shatter. But wait! Not to fear, Cinderella has the match. She reveals that favor was in her side-pocket all along!

Here's what I have always wondered about this story. How is it, that the glass slipper was the only thing that stayed the same, while everything else turned back to its original form at midnight? Here's what I derived as a practical point, Favor is simply unexplainable.

As the story comes to a close, Cinderella still takes her seat after producing the other slipper. Now, the fact that she had the other slipper should have been enough, but she takes the time to put on the shoe. Everyone in the room is looking with pregnant anticipation, especially her haters. She knows she is going to be the right match, but she is relishing her moment! After the graceful fitting of the glass slipper, by the prince no doubt, she and he lived happily ever after. THE END!

Though this tale is fictional, it points to a factual component of life...... Haters have and will always exist. They come in many forms. However, never let a Hater stop you from enjoying the opportunities of grace. They will stare disdainfully, say things, or treat you in ways that will make you uncomfortable. So uncomfortable that you don't want to enjoy God's provision. It will take faith, at times, to enjoy divine favor.

Psalms 23:5a is God pulling us boldly forward to enjoy His marvelous advantages. He stands guard, like a good Shepherd, and makes sure we graze on grace without fear and hesitation. While our haters, on the other hand, can only look on with impotent rage, as there is nothing they can do about it!!

Remember! He subdues haters, enabling us to enter our space of grace with confidence....bon appetite!

".....THOU ANOINEST MY HEAD WITH OIL; MY CUP RUNNETH OVER."
(PSALMS 23:5B, C)

When taking care of sheep, a shepherd heavily anoints or applies oil to the sheep's head, nose, and ears. This is done to avoid lice and ticks from burrowing themselves in said areas. On the occasion that insects needle themselves into these sensitive places, it causes the sheep to become disoriented or mentally confused.

We are subject to the same manner of attacks within these sensitive parts. Satan's goal is to keep us disoriented or mentally confused, in order to separate us from our faith in God.

When Satan attacks our:

Minds he is looking to invade our thinking with hostile reasoning that challenges our faith.   2 Corinthians 10:3-5 warns that *"vain imaginations"* will come along with other *"things"* to usurp the knowledge we have about God.

Sense of smell it is our sense of perception that he is after. Perception allows us to confidently recognize the hand of God in our life, without visible manifestation. We are clearly instructed to "walk by faith and not by sight" in 2 Corinthians 5:7. Perception is directly linked to our faith-*a confident declaration of what we believe without seeing*. When the enemy distorts our perception, he causes us to loosen our grip on faith through unbelief. Unbelief and doubt tie God's hand. Consequently, we are then entrenched in the distresses and difficulties of life like quicksand, stuck and eventually swallowed whole.

Ears he is looking to interfere with our ability to hear and recognize divine truth. Our ears are especially important. They expose us to information that is contemplated in our minds, which in turn, strengthens our perception. Romans 10:17 declares *"So then faith cometh by hearing, and hearing by the word of God."* It is our ability to hear and understand the word of God that causes our faith to develop and hold firm. Satan wages war by intruding upon our hearing with warped information.

Now that we know how sensitive these areas are, we, like sheep, have to have them adequately protected. We must apply the power of the Holy Spirit, represented as the "oil", through prayer, fasting, and continued exposure to the preached, taught, and read word of God. It must be so applied that it overflows to capacity. It is this connection and saturation by the Spirit of God, that holds us together, while simultaneously disallowing Satan to disrupt our convictions in Christ.

Remember! The power of God's Spirit will protect our minds, perception and hearing, causing us to continuously hold tight to our faith.

"SURELY GOODNESS AND MERCY SHALL FOLLOW ME ALL THE DAYS OF MY LIFE: AND I WILL DWELL IN THE HOUSE OF THE LORD FOREVER."(PSALMS 23:6)

I have learned, over the years that a successful relationship involves reciprocity. It is not that we do things in order to have things done for us, but we believe our love for one another motivates acts of kindness. Making a cycle of reciprocity inevitable. Although faithfulness to my relationships is not based on this concept, reciprocity helps to tether my faith and remain faithful to that relationship. No one wants to be involved in a relationship that lacks a mutual give and take. That at some point our acts of kindness bares mutuality.

I believe we can live with a level of expectation that our acts of adoration, which are done out of love for God, will somehow reap the benefits of divine acts of grace. Inevitably, engaging us in a cycle of reciprocity. There is an old song that explains it as such: When the praises go up the blessings come down. Further still is the prayer that Jabez prayed 1 Chronicles 4:9, 10. When he uses the word "bless" me indeed. The New Strongs Exhaustive Concordance of the bible provides the definition 'Vice Versa" as a Hebrew of the word "bless". Here's how we have used vice versa in a sentence. "I will pick you up tonight but tomorrow…vice versa" In others words there will be an exchange actions that takes place. I'll do this, and you will do something in return. Jabez petition to God said "that as I bless you, I would like you to bless me back. And here is what I would like you to do." At the end of his request we read the words *"And God granted him what he requested."*

It should be no mystery to us then that David believes the kindness and faithfulness of God would pursue him *"all the days of his life"* because of David's desire to *"dwell in the house of the Lord forever."*

If we study David's life, we will find conjoining thoughts. Psalms 27:4

"One thing have I desired of the Lord, that will I seek after; that I may dwell in the house of the Lord all the days of my life to behold the beauty of the Lord and to inquire in his temple."

I work downtown and am constantly exposed to the homeless who spend their entire day pleading for financial assistance. Some strategically place themselves right in front of banking institutions, in hopes of increasing their chances of receiving money.

When the bible describes David's desire for the presence of God in Psalms 27:4, it is as one who is begging, so he strategically places himself in the house of God to have his desire met.

He goes on to say in Ps. 92:13, 14:

"13.Those that be planted in the house of the LORD shall flourish in the court of our God, 14. They shall still bring forth fruit in old age; they shall be fat and flourishing."

It is clear, David understood that desire for God's presence offered eternal rewards. He specifically states, that if we are thoroughly immersed in the house of God, like a seed that is planted, we "will be fat and flourishing". Sounds like grace to me!

This is the moment where we are encouraged to *Remember* a clear and practical point of how The Good Shepherd extends care, to fortify our grasp on faith…so here it is: God uses reciprocity to strengthen our hold on faith in Him.

Final thoughts:

We are now at the conclusion of the whole matter Faith, which is this: Never, never, never, never, never, and I do mean NEVER! Give up your Confidence in God.
It is our assured belief in Him that will navigate us through the distresses, difficulties and distractions of life. Should we struggle with our faith, God is there to add strength.

I hope you have enjoyed reading these points of encouragement, to hold tight to your faith, as much as I have had the pleasure to write them.
God bless!

ABOUT THE AUTHOR

A dynamic speaker, Nikki Crutchfield, enjoys researching the scriptures for biblical truths that enable her to live life successfully as a Christian. Blogging allowed her to transform her research into a narrative to be read by all. Nikki resides in Beltsville, Md. with her husband and two teenage sons. You can follow her on periscope @hiswordsnwisdom, Facebook words-n-wisdom, get access to her blogs on WordPress @God reminds me, and keep up-to- date with her ongoing projects by checking in @ www.wordsnwisdom.com

www.ingramcontent.com/pod-product-compliance
Lightning Source LLC
Chambersburg PA
CBHW031526040426

42445CB00009B/415